# BODY
# MANNERS

## JOSH PLATTNER

Consulting Editor, Diane Craig, M.A./Reading Specialist

**Sandcastle**

An Imprint of Abdo Publishing
abdopublishing.com

# abdopublishing.com

Published by Abdo Publishing, a division of ABDO, PO Box 398166, Minneapolis, Minnesota 55439. Copyright © 2016 by Abdo Consulting Group, Inc. International copyrights reserved in all countries. No part of this book may be reproduced in any form without written permission from the publisher. SandCastle™ is a trademark and logo of Abdo Publishing.

Printed in the United States of America, North Mankato, Minnesota

062015
092015

Editor: Alex Kuskowski
Content Developer: Nancy Tuminelly
Cover and Interior Design and Production: Mighty Media, Inc.
Photo Credits: Shutterstock

**Library of Congress Cataloging-in-Publication Data**

Plattner, Josh, author.

 Body manners / Josh Plattner ; consulting editor, Diane Craig, M.A./Reading Specialist.

    pages cm. -- (Manners)

 Audience: PreK to grade 3.

 ISBN 978-1-62403-714-6

1. Etiquette for children and teenagers--Juvenile literature.  I. Title.

 BJ1857.C5P53 2016

 395.1'22--dc23

                 2014046366

## SandCastle™ Level: Transitional

SandCastle™ books are created by a team of professional educators, reading specialists, and content developers around five essential components—phonemic awareness, phonics, vocabulary, text comprehension, and fluency—to assist young readers as they develop reading skills and strategies and increase their general knowledge. All books are written, reviewed, and leveled for guided reading, early reading intervention, and Accelerated Reader™ programs for use in shared, guided, and independent reading and writing activities to support a balanced approach to literacy instruction. The SandCastle™ series has four levels that correspond to early literacy development. The levels are provided to help teachers and parents select appropriate books for young readers.

EMERGING · BEGINNING · **TRANSITIONAL** · FLUENT

# CONTENTS

# BODY
# MANNERS

Manners are great!

They are important.

Use good body manners.

# BODY BASICS

Brush your teeth. Keep your hands clean. Wash your face too!

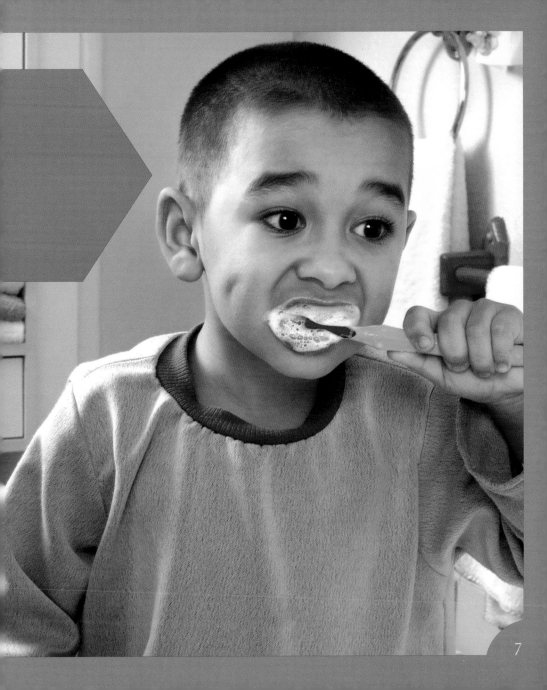

# STAND RIGHT

Ginny stands up
straight. She does not
**slouch**. She says "hello"
to others.

# SPEAKING UP

Amy talks to her friends. She does not **mumble**. She keeps her voice down. She does not yell.

# SNEEZE SAFE

Cover your nose when you **sneeze**. Blow your nose in private. Use a **tissue**. Wash your hands after sneezing.

# COVERED COUGHING

Mark **coughs** into his arm. He does not cough on his hands. He washes his hands after coughing.

# BATHROOM BREAKS

Jon asks to be excused.

He uses the bathroom.

He washes his hands.

He dries them too.

# PERSONAL SPACE

Keep your hands to
yourself. Don't get too
close to others. Ask if
you are too close.

# DON'T DO THAT!

Don't pick your nose. Don't talk when someone else is talking. Do not hit other people.

# KEEP IT UP!

Always practice good body manners. Can you think of more? What else could you do?

# GLOSSARY

**cough** - the act or sound of suddenly forcing air out of your lungs.

**mumble** - to speak quietly and unclearly so it is hard for other people to hear.

**slouch** - a way of standing or sitting with the head and shoulders hunched.

**sneeze** - the act or sound of suddenly forcing air out through your nose or mouth.

**tissue** - a thin paper used to wipe one's face or blow one's nose.